KING PHILIP'S WAR: THE NATIVES VS. THE ENGLISH COLONISTS

US History Lessons
Children's American Revolution History

Speedy Publishing LLC

40 E. Main St. #1156

Newark, DE 19711

www.speedypublishing.com

Copyright 2017

The first major war between Native Americans and European settlers in North America is sometimes called King Philip's War. What happened and who was King Philip? Let's find out!

A WAR FOR LAND AND A WAY OF LIFE

King Philip's War, or The First Indian War, took place in New England from 1675 to 1678. English colonists, and their allies from the Mohegan and Pequot tribes, fought an alliance of Native Americans determined to stop the settlers taking over the tribes' traditional lands.

MAP SHOWING NATIVE AMERICAN TRIBAL AREAS

METACOMET (1638-1676, OR KING PHILIP)

The Wampanoag, Nipmuck, Podunk, Narragansett and Nashaway tribes followed the lead of the Wampanoag chief Metacomet, nicknamed "King Philip" by the colonists.

BEFORE THE WAR

The Pilgrims created a settlement at what is now Plymouth, Massachusetts in 1620. Without help from the Wampanoag tribe under Massasoit, the Pilgrims would not have survived their first year.

The coastal areas of New England seemed like an empty wilderness to the colonists, but the territory had long been home to many tribes. Those tribes had been largely wiped out by diseases brought to the New World by European fishermen and whalers in the years leading up to 1620.

PLIMOTH PLANTATION IN PLYMOUTH, MA

Relations were generally peaceful between the new arrivals and the original residents, but the tribes began to get worried as European settlements and farmlands took over more and more territory the Native Americans had traditionally used for hunting and farming. The colonists made many promises not to take over too much land, and again and again they broke their promises.

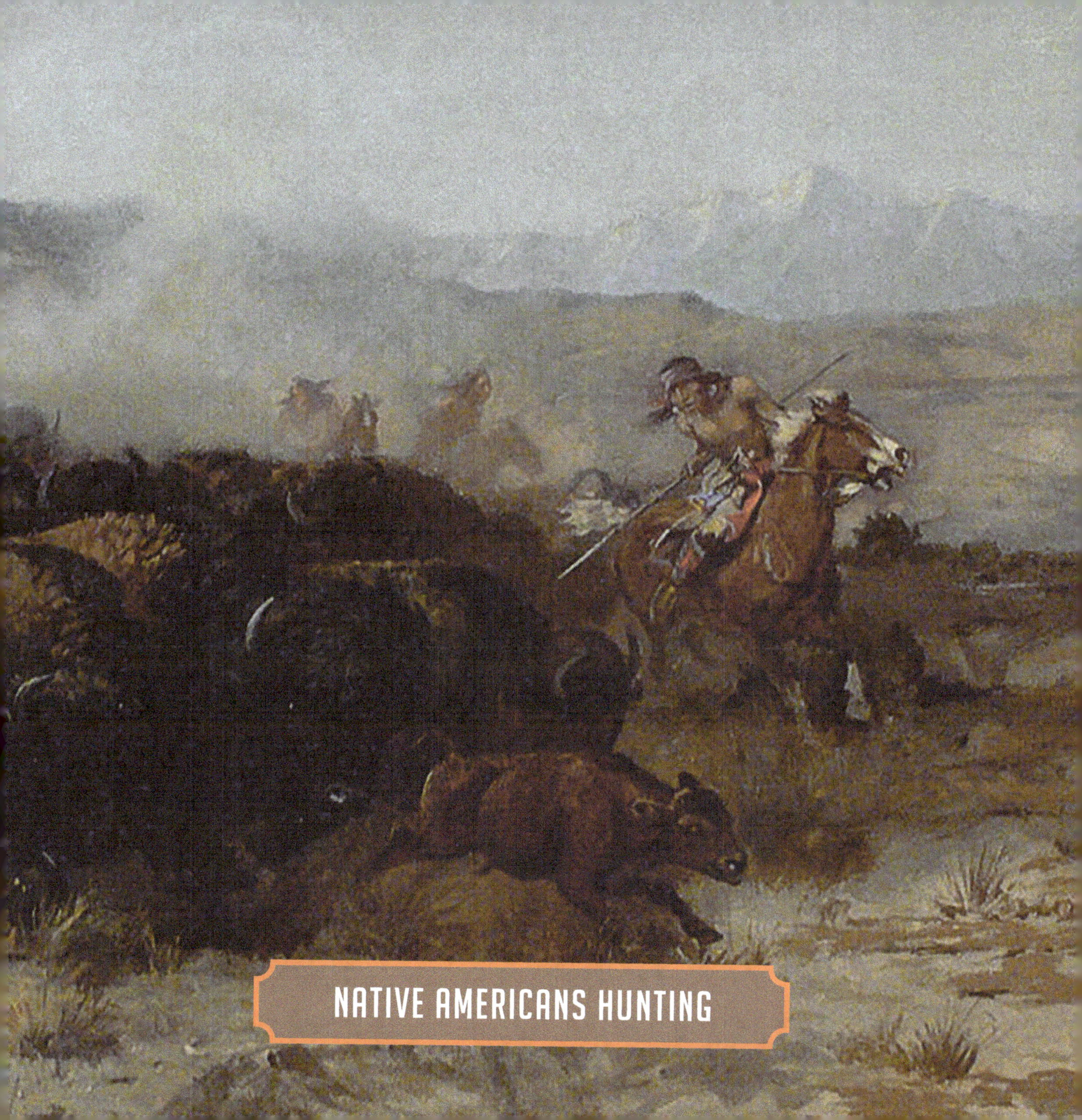

NATIVE AMERICANS HUNTING

Some of the colonists, like Roger Williams in Rhode Island, had good and respectful relations with the Native Americans. Many others, however, thought that the "Indians" were not quite human, and were a danger that should be wiped out.

RETURN OF ROGER WILLIAMS

TATUE OF THE MASSASOIT GREAT SACHEM OF THE WAMPANOAGS

Finally, Metacomet, son of Massasoit and now chief of the Wampanoags, became convinced that the tribes should drive the settlers out of New England, or they would lose everything. In 1675 he said that it would be better to die than to continue to live until he had no country left.

Under Metacomet, the tribes began preparing for war. They even formally sold some of their land in order to be able to buy guns and ammunition.

THE SPARKS OF WAR

One problem between the two peoples was that the settlers' cattle and other animals would regularly get into the fields of corn and other crops planted by the tribes, causing great damage.

CATTLE

WAMPANAOG MAN

After some cattle near Bristol, Rhode Island damaged Wampanoag corn fields, some fighters killed the cattle. In response, a settler shot and killed one of the Wampanoag.

Soon after, in Massachusetts, the settlers put three Wampanoag men to death. In response, Metacomet ordered a full attack on Swansea. Many colonists were killed and the city was burned.

ATTACKS AND AMBUSHES

During 1675 there were attacks by each side on the other. If the Europeans burned a tribe's village, the tribes would respond by attacking, and often burning, a colonial village.

TRIBES BURNING COLONIAL VILLAGE

WOODEN FORT

The Wampanoags, joined by Nipmucks, attacked Brookfield, Massachusetts with a large force in August, 1675. Brookfield had been settled in 1660 and probably had fewer than 100 residents. The attackers killed many soldiers and burned the whole town except for a small wooden fort.

They were close to burning that last refuge of the settlers when a rain storm put out the fire. Soon afterwards soldiers arrived from other towns and forced the tribes to withdraw.

The tribes then attacked settlements along the Connecticut River valley, and forced the colonists to abandon settlements like Deerfield.

CONNECTICUT RIVER VALLEY

BATTLE OF BLOODY BROOK

They ambushed a troop of English soldiers, killing more than 70 in at what is now known as Bloody Brook.

Attacks continued into the autumn. When colonists took some children of the Agawam tribe as hostages, to try to keep that tribe out of the war, the Agawams responded by burning the town of Springfield.

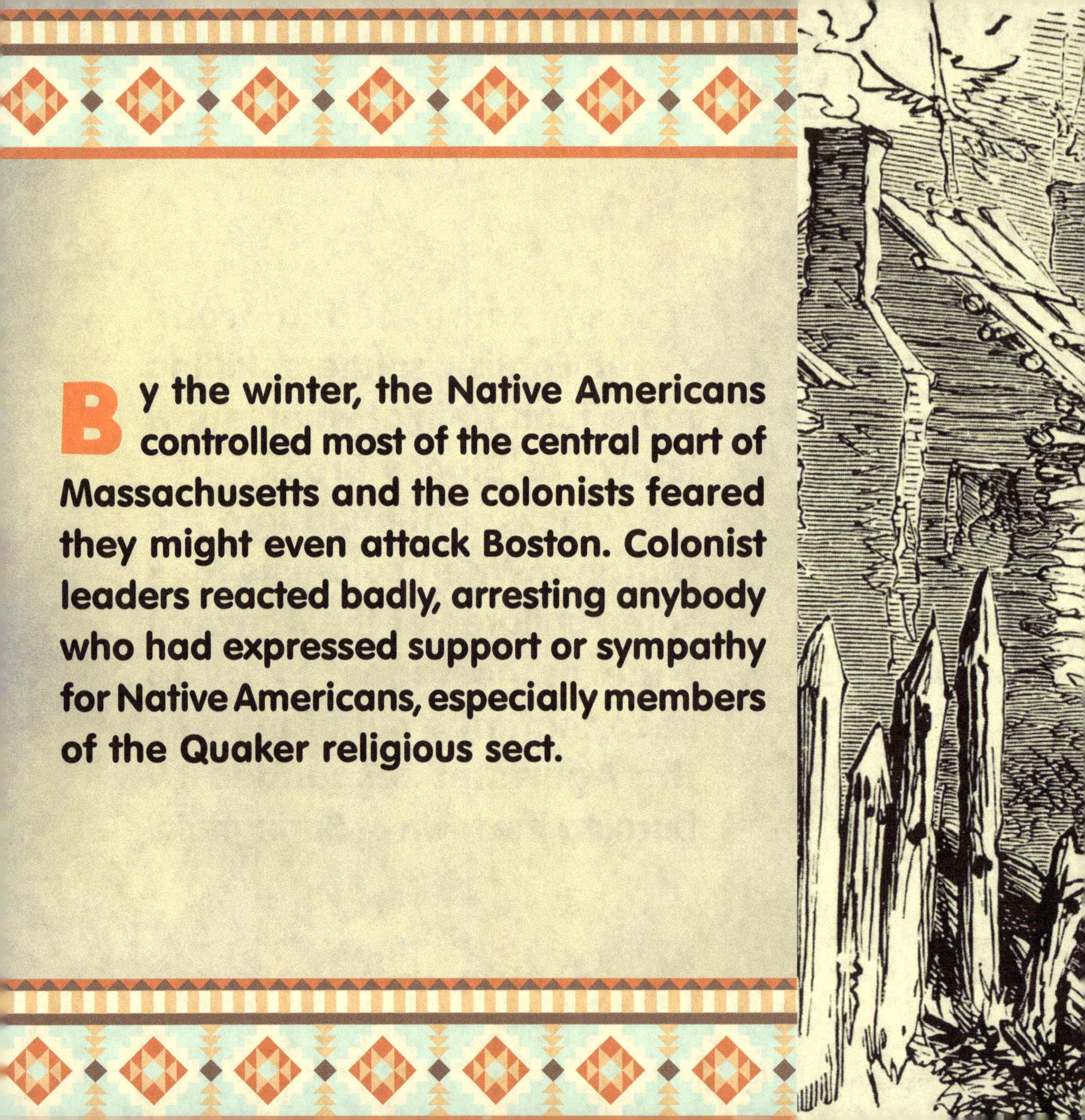

By the winter, the Native Americans controlled most of the central part of Massachusetts and the colonists feared they might even attack Boston. Colonist leaders reacted badly, arresting anybody who had expressed support or sympathy for Native Americans, especially members of the Quaker religious sect.

On the other side, the tribes were short on food because they had spent their summer at war instead of hunting and harvesting. They had lost many fighters and did not have the resources to continue a long war.

THE SETTLERS STRIKE BACK

In December of 1675 the colonists decided they had to do something big. They decided to attack and destroy a major tribal center. Oddly, they chose to attack the Narragansetts, a tribe that had lived peacefully with the Europeans since the first settlers had arrived, and that up to that point had not been involved in the war.

COLONIALS ATTACKING A TRIBE

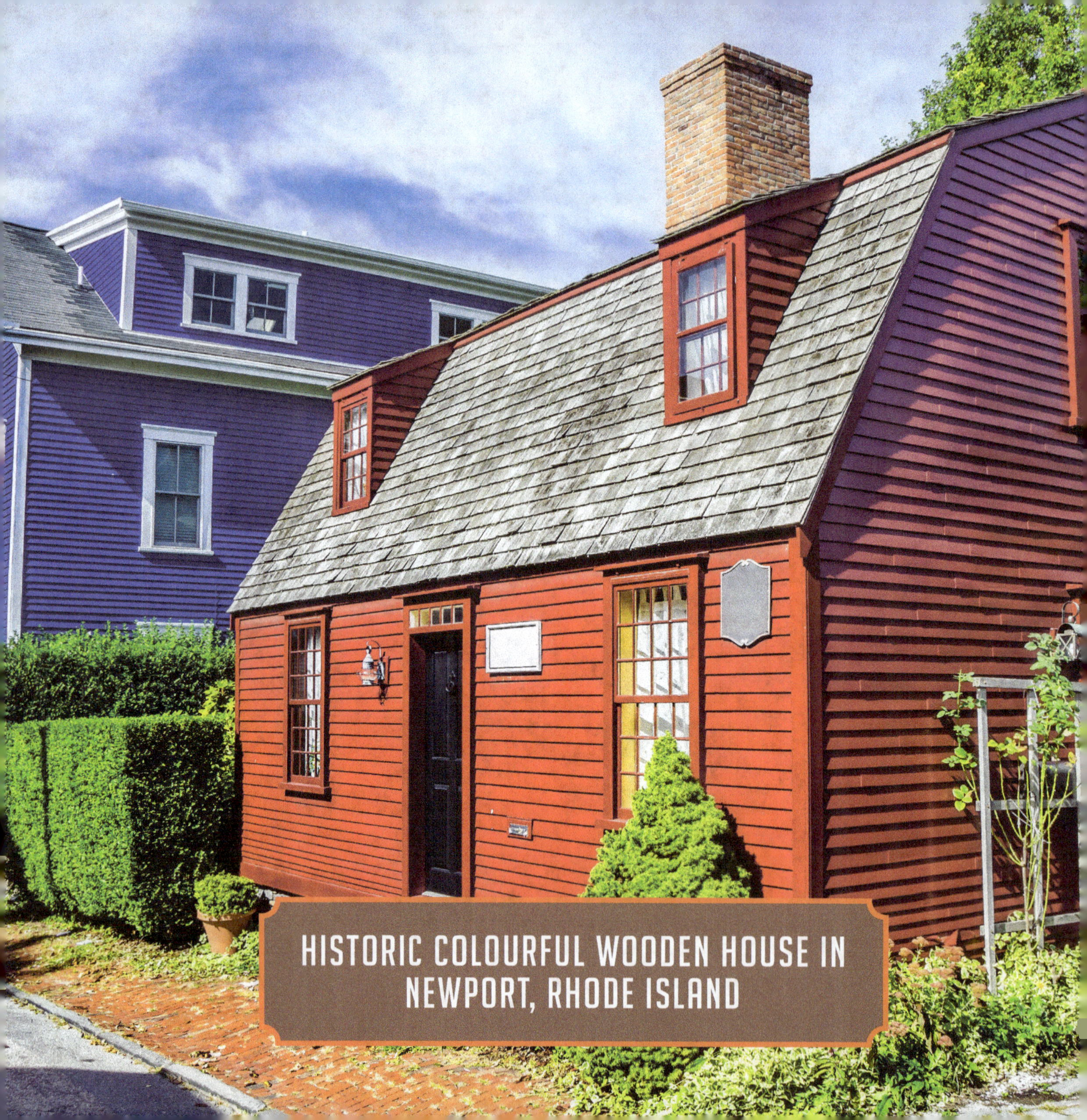HISTORIC COLOURFUL WOODEN HOUSE IN
NEWPORT, RHODE ISLAND

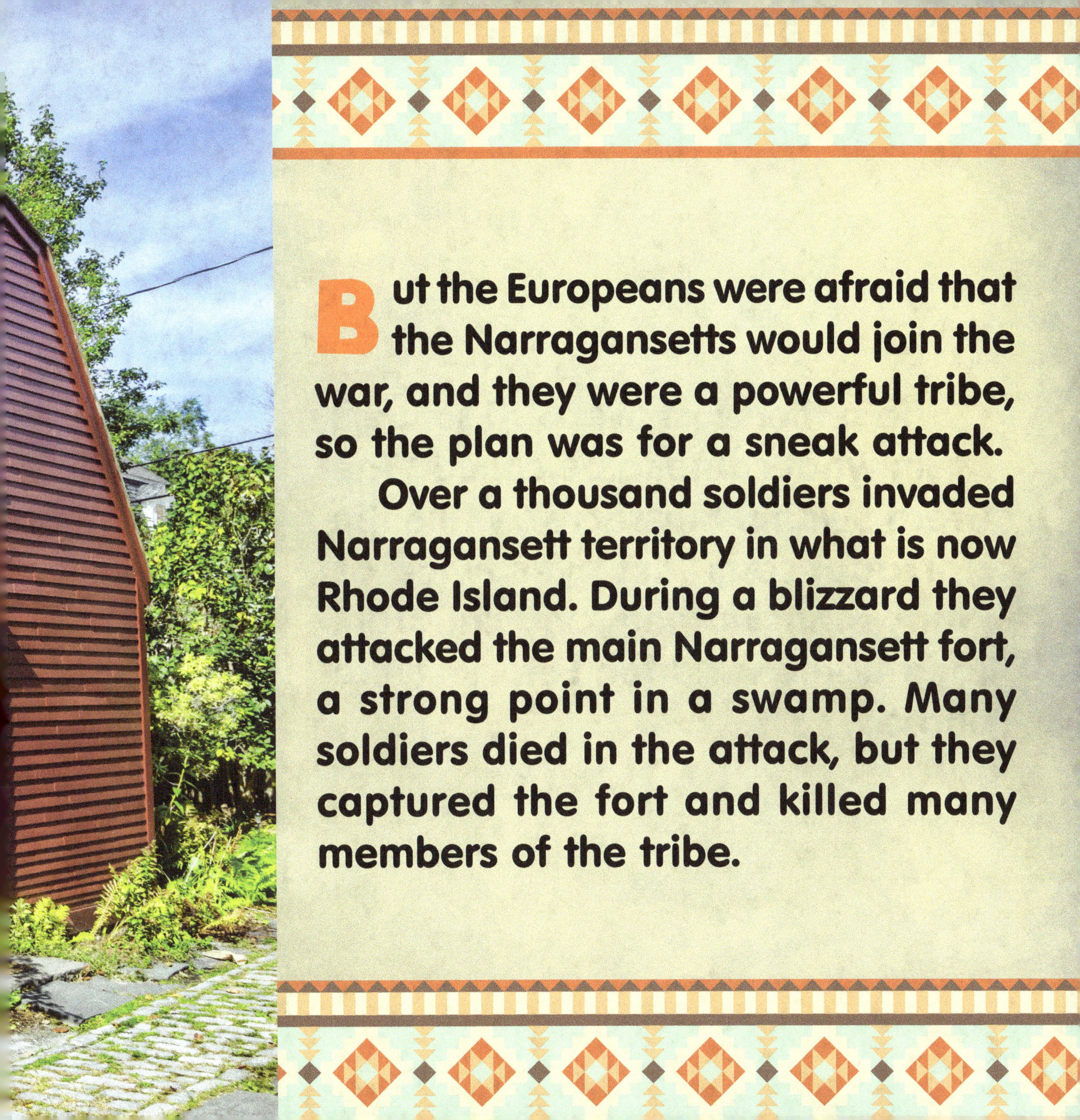

But the Europeans were afraid that the Narragansetts would join the war, and they were a powerful tribe, so the plan was for a sneak attack.

Over a thousand soldiers invaded Narragansett territory in what is now Rhode Island. During a blizzard they attacked the main Narragansett fort, a strong point in a swamp. Many soldiers died in the attack, but they captured the fort and killed many members of the tribe.

The settlers lost over 300 soldiers in what came to be called "The Great Swamp Massacre", while the Narragansetts lost over twice as many men, women, and children. Their homes and food stocks were burned.

GREAT SWAMP FIGHT MONUMENT

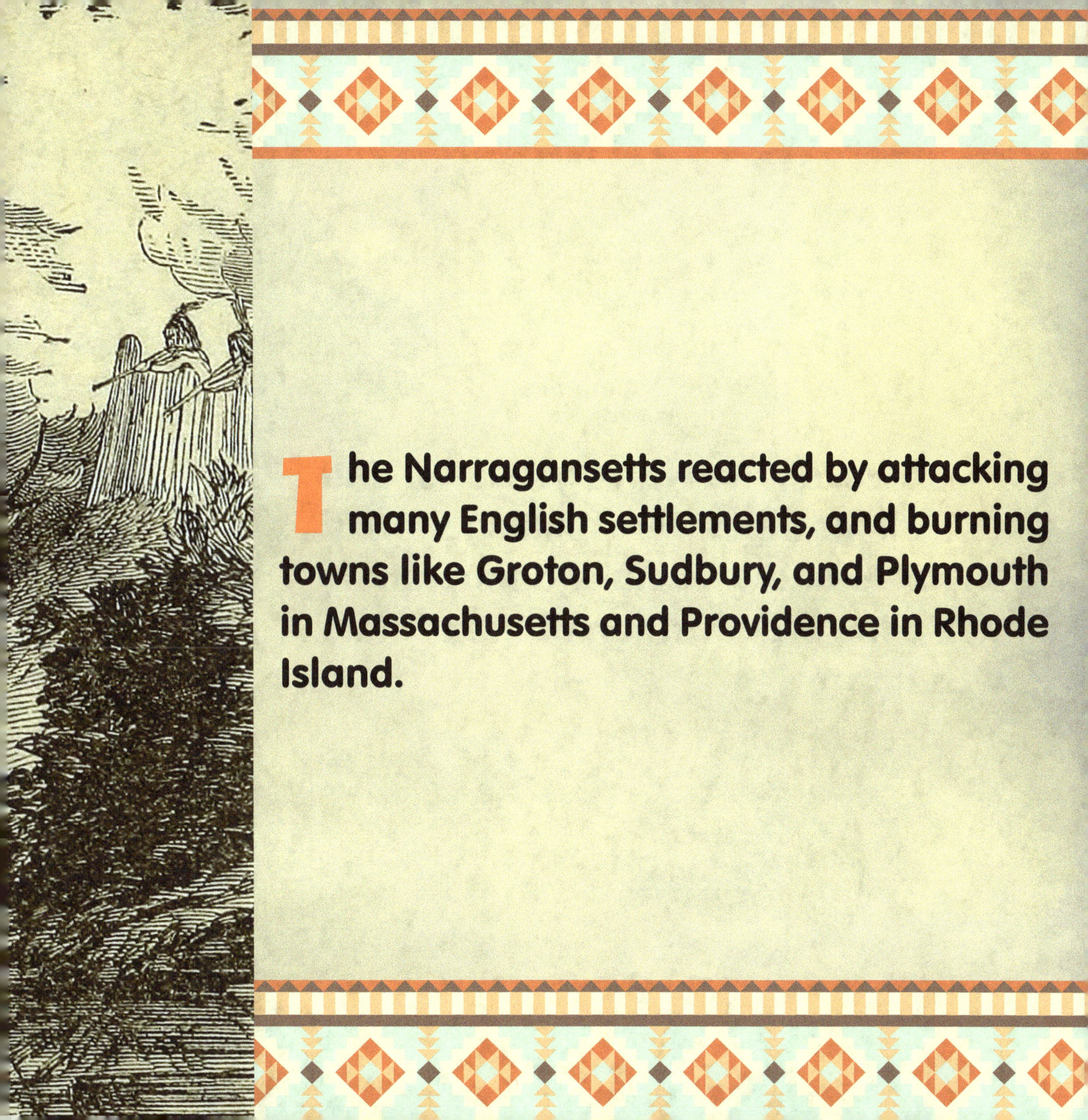

The Narragansetts reacted by attacking many English settlements, and burning towns like Groton, Sudbury, and Plymouth in Massachusetts and Providence in Rhode Island.

However, the Narragansetts, and all the tribes were running short of supplies and especially ammunition, while the organization of the settlers was improving.

NATIVE AMERICAN WEAPONS

WIGWAM

THE END OF THE WAR

A surprise raid on Metacomet's main camp on the Connecticut River in 1676 helped to break the tribes' control of the central Massachusetts region. Many of the native people were killed in their wigwams, or drowned while trying to cross the river to escape the attack. The main battle force of the Wampanoags and Nipmucks was destroyed, and the tribal alliance started to fall apart.

While many Native Americans continued fighting, others fled north or west away from the settlers' area and into the territories of other tribes. These tribes did not always welcome them.

Metacomet retreated to Swansea with a small force of fighters and tried to continue the war. Through the summer he continued to attack small villages and farms, but now the colonists' response was stronger. The remaining Native American fighters were able to inflict much less damage than they had in the previous year.

NATIVE AMERICAN WARRIOR

THE DEATH OF METACOMET

A force under Benjamin Church, who had led the sneak attack on the Narragansetts, pursued Metacomet and his small band, and finally caught up with him near Mount Hope, Rhode Island. Metacomet was killed in a battle there. The settlers cut off his head and stuck it on the top of a pole at Newport, Rhode Island. This horrible trophy of the war stayed on display there for over twenty years.

KEY POINTS ABOUT THE WAR

Here are some details of King Philip's War:

- Metacomet was nicknamed "King Philip" after the king of Macedon who was the father of Alexander the Great.
- The colonists got almost no help from England during the war.

STATUE OF ALEXANDER THE GREAT

CAPTIVITY OF MRS. ROWLANDS

- **Half of the ninety towns of New England were attacked during the war.**
- **Twelve towns were completely destroyed. Brookfield, for instance, was burned to the ground and was not rebuilt for twelve years.**
- **Mary Rowlandson was captured in the attack and destruction of the town of Lancaster, Massachusetts, in the winter of 1676. She was a captive for six weeks until she was ransomed. Her story of the battle and of her time as a prisoner is some of the best first-hand reporting of King Philip's War.**

- **John Alderman, a Native American fighting on the side of the colonists, shot and killed Metacomet.**
- **Although Metacomet died in the summer of 1676, there were battles in parts of New England until 1678, when a permanent peace treaty was signed.**

THE DEATH OF METACOMET

KING PHILIP'S WAR

CONSEQUENCES OF THE WAR

In terms of the number of people involved on both sides, King Philip's War was one of the bloodiest in American history. At least six hundred colonists and over three thousand Native Americans died in the fighting. Many more Native Americans were taken prisoner and sent into slavery in other colonies.

The colonists had narrowly survived an attack that could have wiped out the English presence in New England. However, it was they who won and it was the native people who lost their traditional lands. The early experiment of settlers and Native Americans living in harmony together was over.

NEW ENGLAND

THE NATIVE AMERICAN EXPERIENCE

Before the Europeans arrived, there were millions of Native Americans in hundreds of tribes living all across North America. The original occupants of the land lost numbers, power, and the ability to live their traditional way of life as the numbers and power of the colonists grew.

Read more about the Native American experience in Baby Professor books like Are Indian Reservations part of the US?, What Happened Before, During and After the Battle of the Little Bighorn?, The Wounded Knee Massacre, and The Heart-Shattering Facts about the Trail of Tears.

Visit

BABY PROFESSOR
EDUCATION KIDS

www.BabyProfessorBooks.com

to download Free Baby Professor eBooks and view
our catalog of new and exciting Children's Books